Instant Fishing

To *look like* a fisherman

Books by Richard Gordon

NOVELS

Doctor in the House
Doctor at Sea
Doctor at Large
Doctor in Love
Doctor and Son
Doctor in Clover
Doctor on Toast
Doctor in the Swim
Doctor on the Boil
Doctor on the Brain
Doctor in the Nude
Doctor on the Job

The Captain's Table
Nuts in May
The Summer of Sir Lancelot
Love and Sir Lancelot
The Facemaker
Surgeon at Arms
The Facts of Life
The Medical Witness
The Sleep of Life
The Invisible Victory
*The Private Life of
    Florence Nightingale*

GENERAL

Good Neighbours
Happy Families
Instant Fishing

BY MARY AND RICHARD GORDON

A Baby in the House

Instant Fishing

Richard Gordon

with drawings by Michael ffolkes

HEINEMANN : LONDON

William Heinemann Ltd
15 Queen Street, Mayfair, London W1X 8BE

LONDON MELBOURNE TORONTO
JOHANNESBURG AUCKLAND

First published 1979
© Richard Gordon Ltd 1979

SBN 434 30255 4

Filmset in 12/14 point Bembo
Printed and bound in Great Britain
by W & J Mackay Limited, Chatham

Contents

Foreword	ix
1. Man *v*. Fish	1
2. Choice of Weapons	15
3. On the Trail of the Trout	35
4. Attack	51
5. The Great Deception	71
6. The Artless Dodger	89
7. Catching Your Fish	101
8. The Inner Angler	115

Foreword

This is a sympathetic guide to fly-fishing for trout. Its foundations are eleven entirely new PRINCIPLES OF INCOMPLEAT ANGLING. Its advice is practical, across the whole subject, from choosing a rod to cooking the catch.

It is for the beginner who can distinguish a trout only because it has a plastic label stuck through it on a fishmonger's slab. He will never become a compleat angler by reading *this* book. But if it encourages him to become an angler at all, I shall have gladly fulfilled my purpose.

I have had almost half a century's experience of incompleat angling. Long ago, I realized that I should never soar—like the lovely full-blown mayfly spinner from its drab, hairy, immature dun—into the enviable golden air of compleation. I have no regrets. No man can look back with regret on a life in which a summer without any angling was like a summer without any sun.

1
Man v. Fish

I

FIRST PRINCIPLE OF INCOMPLEAT ANGLING. *Fly-fishing is Easy. Catching Trout is Difficult.*

* * *

There are four sorts of fishing—
(1) *Coarse Fishing.* Sitting on a small folding stool under an umbrella all winter.
(2) *Sea Fishing.* Windy, muscular and emetic.
(3) *Salmon Fishing.* As expensive as keeping a mistress, but much more frustrating.
(4) *Trout Fishing.* Perfection in angling.

I prescribe trout fishing. I love it, I weary everybody endlessly about it, because—

Unlike (1), being performed on foot rather than on the bum, a day's fishing is a day's exercise.

Unlike (2), the trout draws its pursuers more intimately than can the cod into the entrancing and reposeful embrace of Nature. It avoids messy messing about in boats, and the relentless inquisitiveness of pier-end holiday-makers on whether you've had a bite yet, mate.

To practitioners of (3), the arrival of a salmon in their lives is an event as sensational as the birth of their children. They appear similarly slighted if all their friends fail to photograph, admire and fuss over the little stranger. With (4), given a little practice and luck, even the most incompleat angler manages to bring home *something*. His trout may be the size of a tinned sardine, but he can grill it and eat it for breakfast with the piquant sauce of self-satisfaction, the reward through the ages of the huntsman and the cannibal.

Trout angling is the perfect tranquillizer. It is addictive, but non-toxic and never fatal. The possibility of a trout exposing itself, or more excitingly endangering itself, the necessity to avoid hooking trees, fences and your own ear-lobes, offers just enough constant interest, and demands just enough constant concentration, to prevent the mind straying in its unkindly way back to the worries and hazards of life. The eternal elusiveness of his prey induces in the trout fisherman a saintly resignation, which may extend to the frustrations and disappointments of the world beyond the river bank.

"He would praise God that he had spent that day free from worldly trouble," the entirely compleat angler Izaak Walton wrote about his fellow-fisher, the Dean of St Paul's. Lean and white-bearded, beatifically gleaming with serenity, Dean Nowel today looks down upon the dining dons of Brasenose, Oxford, not in ecclesiastical pomp but surrounded by his fishing tackle. "He died 13 Feb. 1601, being aged ninety-five years," records Izaak Walton. "His age neither impaired his hearing, nor dimmed his eyes, nor weakened his memory, nor made any of the faculties of his mind weak or useless. It is said that Angling and temperance were great causes of these blessings."

Izaak Walton lived until 1683, four months after a ninetieth birthday on which he found himself "in perfect memory, for which praised be God." Canon Greenwell, his fame freshened each returning season with his fly "Greenwell's Glory," lasted two months short of reaching ninety-eight in 1918. G E M Skues (a name essential for all incompleat anglers to memorize) lived within a week of ninety-one, to August 1949. Arthur Ransome remained among the compleatest of modern anglers until he was eighty-three in the summer of 1967.

Trout fishing is admittedly not among the scientific reasons for a nimble longevity. But it does not seem to do any harm.

* * *

But the incipient angler is scared stiff of trout fishing.

He is a man definite in his enthusiasm but dubious of his ability. The man whose fancy is taken by the tackle-shop — with its rods gleaming like lances, its neat little reels, its flies displayed as temptingly as coloured sweets for children, its waders like bright green cavalry boots, its purposeful waterproof jackets, its little home trout-

But it doesn't seem to do any harm

smokers — and who thinks it would be a good idea if he started getting away from the wife more often. He is the man who wisely perceives that trout fishing promises as good outdoor exercise as golf, with the advantage that you do not have to make conversation with anyone while doing it.

The incipient angler's picture of fly-fishing is a landscape of gentlemen with clipped accents and beautifully-cut tweeds, casting equally well-dressed dry flies at thoroughbred trout, from the close-mown banks of soft-spoken streams round the edges of Salisbury Plain. The scene appears as remote socially and stylishly from coarse fishing as a Gainsborough from the family snaps.

Like Changing the Guard and Ascot week, this sparkle of grandeur may still be glimpsed down the light-years from the Edwardian Age. The finest trout fishing in the world lies in southern England between the White Horse Hills and the Dorset Downs. Among this hundred-mile succession of amiable green slopes wander the famous chalk streams of the Test, the Wiltshire Avon, the Wylye and the Kennet — the Lord's, Twickenham, Wimbledon and Hickstead of fly-fishing, and equally unattainable by the casual sportsman.

Luckily for the present generation, the pleasures of fly-fishing, like those of listening to classical music, travelling abroad, or enjoying out-of-season green peas and carefree sex, have been lavishly disseminated by the blindfold philanthropy of applied science.

This is because the trout, like the out-of-work

actor, will provide entertainment anywhere at least for one summer season. Its performance needs only a gentle flow of cool, unpolluted water to a depth of six feet, with a few holes to serve as sun-shelters. It likes a fringe of trees for shade, and to harbour flies. Like the seedy actor, the trout must still eat, though willing in the circumstances to forgo reproduction.

Our countryside has become peppered with shallow little lakes, where kindly farmers and landowners have dammed streams in marshy fields, or diverted them into bulldozed dells, for the pleasure of a few "rods". (The most incompleat angler must remember to call a fisherman a rod, as a shooter a gun and a Q C a silk.) Mill houses may now shelter more company directors than millers, but their millponds sustain more trout. Some enthusiasts even create trout ponds in their back gardens, which is an extra on the water rates.

These are the amateur playing grounds of trout angling. The professional pitches are made from worked-out gravel pits and quarries, or the vast reservoirs which lie as watery monuments to civilized man's prodigality.

* * *

Trout breed naturally in midwinter, stimulated by the fall in temperature. The female twists over the gravel on the gently-rising lip of a pool, where it senses currents passing downwards into the river-bed. The fish uses the water-pressure of its movements to hollow out a nest. (Fishes' nests are always "redds" to compleat anglers, who share the impish delight of schoolboys in their slang, and confuse incipient anglers with several different names for everything. It is needful for the incompleat angler to learn *all* these by heart.) The male trout meanwhile performs a figure-of-eight love dance above, before settling down to quiver beside her, fin to fin.

Spawning need not be done in Nature's untidy way. The same effect can be achieved in fish-farms, efficiently and hygienically, as the babies born from bottles in Aldous Huxley's *Brave New World*.

Like squeezing out toothpaste, the fish-farmer strips the female trout of eggs and the male of sperm ("milt" to compleat anglers, who sex trout like chickens into hens and cocks). He mixes eggs and milt with a little water in a basin, as if making a sago pudding, then hatches them in neat little plastic boxes on the river-bed, or in tiers of antiseptic-impregnated trays. The young are never called fish, but successively alevins, fry, fingerlings, underyearlings and yearlings. The infant mortality is terrible.

When one or two years old, and ten or twelve inches long, the trout are dispatched in early spring to stock and reinforce the artificial lakes and reservoirs. They are transported by tanker lorry, like the milk or the Guinness. Fishery managers often slip in a few of eighteen inches or more, just for fun. Even the best fisheries stock up from their own stewponds. Some fish take a more direct route to the plate, being served in expensive restaurants as *Truite au bleu*. In times of glut, they end with the indignity of appearing cut-price in newspaper, with chips.

The survival rate of these recruits in the anglers' hands recalls the infantryman on the Somme. But you must not be discouraged by disparagement of "the put-and-take method" of trout fishing. It brings the fun of the sport to incompleat anglers, all of whom live in large and uncomfortable towns. And it brings the excitement of a catch to the utterly incompleat ones like myself, who cast our lines with the subtlety of launching the lifeboat, lose our flies in the long grass and our net in the water, and find ourselves on far too good terms with the landlords of the riverside pubs.

* * *

The shelves of volumes on trout fishing already outstretch the lifetime of the most aged and bookish angler. (One read all through *The Happy Hooker,* waiting for the interesting bit, about fishing.) These publications are of two sorts, romantic fiction and science fiction.

In the romances, a muslin of cloud filters an over-benevolent sun, a breeze like a cherub's breath blows conveniently upstream, at dusk the flies swarm as thick as fog and the trout all suffer from gluttony and suicidal tendencies. The heroes of these works net two- and three-pounders with the nonchalance of actresses accepting compliments. Only total darkness ends their gleeful sport, when they stagger under their load to a handy inn of great charm and modest prices, to sup in superb simplicity and yarn with fellow-fishers over whisky-and-sodas long into the night, on fish caught and fish lost, and the eternal fickleness of Nature.

These books overlook snow in May, tree-bending gales in June, barbed-wire fences seemingly magnetic to the hook, tangled nylon casts in ill-tempered fingers, the begrudging and overpriced hotels, the surly farmers, the bulls, the infuriatingly bigger fish caught by equally incompetent anglers, and worst of all the fishing bores (less tormenting than the fishing boasters, who must be upended in the water and held by the ankles until overcome by silence). I read this charming escapism all winter, alternating with cricket books in which everyone scores centuries and hat-tricks, and all Yorkshiremen are genial, approachable repositories of homespun wisdom.

The science fiction is sold as instruction manuals. It discusses the Spey and Wye casts, the voluntary and the induced take, and has always a lot to say about nymphing. Such expert works are for the compleat angler, or the man grimly determined to become one.

The danger to the incompleat angler is having his interest aroused by the first kind of book and as quickly flattened by the second. The average angler, like the average doctor, anyway picks up his practical tips from watching his fellows.

It is the fisherman not the fish who demands the author's sympathetic concentration. Compare this brace of God's creatures, sharing a few square feet of peaceful, silent countryside, locked in an atavistic struggle, quivering with cunning and savagery.

The trout is a foot-long three-year-old. Its senses are hair-triggered, its reflexes explosive. Three-fifths of it is solid muscle (which is the bit the man is hopefully planning to eat).

The man who has taken up angling after half an admirable lifetime behind a desk or a workbench is the equivalent of an old trout pushing five (some trout grow as old as seven, a few in nutritious lakes reach thirteen — you tell their age from the rings on their scales, like the age of a tree). The man has become a hunter. He has thrown himself back uncountable generations to the Stone Age. And all he does to equip himself for this leap into the abyss of anthropology is to buy a waterproof deerstalker hat.

The summer world without his glasses is a golden Turneresque blur. His nose is calloused with acrid urban smells. An ear which has mastered even British Rail's station announcements cannot tell the plop of a rising trout from a cow pulling its hoof out of the mud. After years of traversing nothing more obstructive than the pile of a good Wilton, he stumbles painfully among the nettles and brambles, soaked because he has misread the weather and sitting on his sandwiches. He is overweight, pitiably vulnerable to sunburn and hay fever, so hamfisted he cannot rewire a light plug without losing the little brass screws for ever on the floor. And he has no hair. I know this physical picture to be a true likeness, because I started in the same state myself.

My aim is transmitting to such a man the valuable art of *how to look like a fly-fisherman* (from a distance).

You may complain there is no point in paying out good money for a book on trout fishing which does not teach you how to catch fish.

"May I complain? There is no point in taking out of the public library a book on trout fishing which does not teach you how to catch fish."

"Exactly. But just looking *like a fly-fisherman — or a golfer or a cricketer or a pop singer — is important. Going through the right motions, plus some luck, may win success and admiration."*

"It seems to me a strange principle on which to base your instruction."

"On the contrary. It is the principle underlying the training of medical students. In five short years, they can be taught only how to resemble doctors and prevented from killing people."

"I was forgetting you were an incompleat doctor, too. Well, another thing. Your advice seems all directed to the man. What about the woman?"

"She doesn't need it. Her natural patience, her skill at fiddly handiwork, her almost inescapable schooling in Nature-study, her disdain of aggressive competitiveness, endows every woman with the qualities of a very compleat angler indeed."

"That was nice."

"Thank you."

Angling for salmon may be the symphony of fishing, sea angling the brass band, coarse fishing the jazz. Trouting is the chamber music. If you are playing for your own enjoyment, the level of competence is secondary. Comfortable mediocrity is the best attainment in any sport. It brings the companionship and the satisfaction, without the aggravating and exhausting necessity of living up to your excellence.

2
Choice of Weapons

2

A Little Natural History

Three hundred and fifty million years ago, it was a very dry season.

The freshwater fish lay gasping everywhere on parched river beds. They had been overtaken by the Devonian Period, one of the series of natural disasters which tempered our evolving earth, an age of vast floods followed by withering droughts. It produced the red sandstone of Bideford Bay, and is called "The Age of Fishes", because they were top creatures in a world shared only with mussels and sponges.

But one of the species *had* to survive. Someone had to illustrate the ingenious principles of Darwinism. The fittest fish in the evolutionary struggle were the *crossopterygians,* which compleat Greek scholars will recognize as meaning "fringed fin".

These fringed fins were toughened with rudimentary bones and lobed like paddles. They can be seen upon the most famous crossopterygian of all — the coelacanth, which got into the newspapers by allowing itself to be caught in 1952 off the Comoro Islands to the north of Madagascar, when it should have been as extinct as the dinosaur. Silvery, oval, stubby-tailed, the size of a meat salver, it can be seen just inside the front door of the Natural History Museum in South Kensington.

The crossopterygians dragged themselves up the arid banks on their stubby fins, to cross the shrivelled countryside in search of a lingering pool or puddle, like piscine dachshunds. Some were lucky. They wriggled back joyfully into familiar watery surroundings with a primeval gurgle of, "I'm all right, Jack." The others simply could not find a drop. In the end they gave up looking, and resigned themselves to living permanently on dry land.

They had terrible problems of integration. Air is feeble fare if you breathe with gills, and ridiculous for keeping you upright. The swing of temperature gave everyone a perspiration problem. Some crossopterygians grew nimbler on their fins, and ate the others.

Once the rear fins became sound enough to stand on, the front pair were released for catching fleas, hurling spears or cooking the dinner. These landbound crossopterygians later postulated the theories of gravity and relativity, painted the Sistine Chapel, wrote *Hamlet* and Beethoven's Fifth Symphony and invented psychology.

They also analyzed the earth's chemicals, rearranging their molecules into an enormous variety of new ones for their own insatiable needs. When descendants of the lucky and unlucky water-hunting crossopterygians meet today, they are connected by nine feet of high-density fibre-glass, ten yards of plastic-coated chemically-impregnated nylon braid, two and a half feet of transparent nylon filament and a small steel hook.

The difficulties of effecting this introduction have had two effects. They have spawned a worldwide tackle industry with yearly profits of many million pounds, and they make any angler first entering a tackle-shop feel like a fish out of water.

* * *

The theory of catching trout is simple.

The fly must flutter on the water to breed. The fish must eat the fly to live. The man catches the fish by imitating the fly by remote control.

The theory may be executed in three ways—
(1) *Dry Fly-fishing*. An imitation fly is placed *upon* the surface of the water. Practised by all compleat anglers.
(2) *Wet Fly-fishing*. An imitation fly is placed *below* the surface of the water. A method severely looked down upon by every dry fly-fisherman.
(3) *Nymphing*. An imitation fly is placed *below* the surface of the water *by a dry fly-fisherman*.

The equipment for catching fish by all three stratagems is almost identical.

There are six essentials.

(1) The Rod

"First, let your rod be light, and very gentle," advised Izaak Walton — which, like everything else he wrote, is worth remembering by even the compleatest contemporary angler.

Izaak Walton would fish as readily with a hand-line on a windle, a little square frame sharing prominence with the Bible in his friend Dean Nowel's Oxford portrait. Or even a forked twig. But rods have been in the anglers' grip a long time. About 700 BC, Homer was working a rod into a simile about Scylla, who lived in her island cave opposite the whirlpool Charybdis and had the habit, fearsomely disgusting even for the Classics, of snatching up passing mariners and eating them raw.

Give me mine angle, commanded the compleatly queenly Cleopatra. *We'll to the river: there,*
My music playing far off, I will betray
Tawny-finn'd fishes; my bended hook shall pierce
Their slimy jaws; and, as I draw them up,
I'll think them every one an Antony,
And say "Ah, ha! you're caught."

Shakespeare took *Antony and Cleopatra* from Plutarch's *Lives,* written in the first century AD (as Izaak Walton took much of *The Compleat Angler* from *The Treatyse of Fysshynge Wyth an Angle,* written by Dame Juliana Berners (or Barnes) in 1496). Plutarch recounts a ceremonious sea-angling expedition in which the love-sick Queen sent divers down to attach fish after fish to Antony's rod, when he was growing as crossly impatient as the rest of us for a bite. After Antony had proudly hauled these into his boat, Cleopatra sportively told her diver to hook on the equivalent of an Egyptian kipper, causing much mirth among his fellow-fishers. A woman like that deserved coming to a bad end.

The home-made rods when Izaak Walton fished were saplings of willow, hazel, blackthorn or ash, dried over charcoal, hollowed with a glowing wire, the butt strapped with iron bands. In the next century, timber of the greenheart and lancewood trees was imported from Guyana, a hard springy wood which stayed popular during two hundred years for fishing-rods, carriage-shafts and croquet-mallets.

Like county cricket and League football, trout-fishing flourished to its present organized state in the warmth of the sun which never set on the British Empire. The Victorians and Edwardians owned beautiful greenheart rods with moulded handles and precise fittings of Birmingham brass, twenty or more feet long. The praiseworthy vigour of the Empire Builders in handling such weighty tackle is not demanded from the modern fisherman, who can pick from three types of rod—

(a) *Split Cane*

The traditional trout rod, now growing outdated. Spilt cane gave more life to the line than could the most massive greenheart. These rods were first made a century ago out of bamboo from Tonkin — *upper* Tonkin, as every very compleat angler will know, where the higher and dryer atmosphere grows a cane tougher than down in the swamp. The bamboo was cut lengthwise, cleared of its woolly pith, and stripped of the hard skin which gave yellow lustre to the Empire Builders' beloved hat-stands, tea-tables and Chinese Chippendale chairs.

The fibrous wood is split into long tapering strips, with a triangular cross-section. Six of these matching pieces are glued together to make a basic rod, a "blank" to the tackle-maker. These are cleaned and varnished or impregnated with resins, exactly as recommended by Izaak Walton, though he himself used linseed-oil and size with red-lead and coal-black.

Top and butt ends are paired, and fitted with rings and a handle from a line of cork circles. You generally get a spare top with each rod you buy.

(b) *Glass*

Almost within the lifetime of some old trout still swimming, a glass rod was appraised by compleat anglers as the golfing professional regarded the hickory-shafted, twine-trailing baffy with which I would insist on projecting both ball and pieces of the fairway in the direction of the hole. These rods were made of ordinary toughened glass, like oven dishes or port decanters. Now they are made of fibreglass, a material more complex, its overlying meshes resembling in structure the tough skin of those insects the fly-fisherman observes so closely from the bank.

The Author in action

The rods are hollow, manufactured more simply than split cane round long steel needles. You do not get a spare top.

(c) *Carbon Fibre*
Featherweight. Used in jet engines. Pure or combined with glass, the most fashionable material for fishing rods.

Which Rod?

Split cane was once cherished for responding sensitively to the flick of the fisherman's wrist, and for best standing the strain of those huge fish which swam through his fantasies. The shopman might still murmur, "Have you considered a Ritz rod, sir?" It is important that the incipient angler avoids reacting to an imagined suggestion of pure gold ferrules and jade rings. This is a rod designed for high-speed casting by the long-lived (1891–1976) Swiss Charles Ritz, a Ritz of the Ritz, but also *un pêcheur à la ligne,* and a useful name for the incompleat angler to drop with G E M Skues'.

Today's incipient angler is wiser to start with a *fibreglass rod*. This is lighter and stiffer than split cane. Many compleat anglers favour fibreglass. They say it provides more power, and therefore the effortless control of yards and yards of line, which excites the unspoken admiration and envy of the rest of us trying to cast accurately beyond the tips of our waders.

All anglers want a *carbon fibre* rod. These jet-black, slimline rods are lighter and stiffer even than fibreglass. They have four advantages, apart from being riverbank status symbols.

(1) They make a day's fishing less tiring.

(2) Their stiffness allows more control over the line.

(3) Carbon fibre recovers its shape quicker. Thus it is easier to cast a faster line.

(4) This quality, plus the rod's smaller diameter, makes casting easier into the wind.

There are four arguments in your choice of rod—

(a) *Price*

The prices of split cane rods vary by about twenty-five per cent. All fibreglass rods are cheaper, about three-fifths of the cost. This is another persuasion of fibreglass for the incipient angler. After a single season he may decide he does not care for the sport, though this is almost inconceivable. Or perhaps some summer evening, when the trout are enjoying their game of tip-and-run at his expense — nudging his fly and vanishing — he will smash his rod in frustration and take up birdwatching. Carbon fibre . . . ay, there's the rub. Almost three times as costly as fibreglass.

(b) *Size*

Modern rods are mostly between nine and ten feet. Smaller ones are designed for narrower streams, longer ones for broad waters. An angler liable to find himself fishing anything from a well-filled ditch to a reservoir should choose a length which suits his height.

(c) *Shopman's Advice*

Anglers in all stages of compleation regard the purchase of even a few flies as an excuse for a chat with the tackle salesman about their own fishing. The sordid commercial transaction occupies only the final few seconds.

This habit is horribly boring for the shop assistants. But at a tackle shop like Farlow's of Pall Mall, they have been bearing it cheerfully since 1840. This is because all tackle-salesmen are fishermen themselves, and therefore the nicest of people. Also, they are keenly desirous of retaining your loyal custom for many, many years, until you finally become a compleated angler. Thus, they will seldom short-sightedly give you unsound or extravagant advice.

Keep your rod clean, prop or hang it upright, and each season check the rings for wear, which damages your line. Rings are replaceable.

(d) *The Most Important Factor*

In the selection of any rod, is simply how you like the feel of it. Take your final fancies on the pavement and swish them about among the pedestrians and traffic. Bus-conductors, burdened shoppers, even traffic wardens will direct to a man attempting to catch trout from the kerbstones remarks which are hardly subtle or unexpected, but always good-humoured. The incipient angler instantly becomes aware of the—

SECOND (PLEASANT) PRINCIPLE OF INCOMPLEAT ANGLING. *The Whole World Loves a Lover and an Angler.*

(2) The Reel

The shopman sells you this with the speedy unconcern of a surgeon snipping out the appendix as an encore to a cholecystectomy. He will always tell you that the reel must balance the rod — with his finger an inch tipwards from the cork handle, rod and reel should stay horizontal.

Izaak Walton tied his horsehair lines to the ring at the tip of his rod. After 1700, the line was passed through this ring, and another ring along the rod, and wound on to a brass "winch" revolving round a centre pin. These were the first trout reels. Salmon fishing needs complicated reels, all invented by prosperous cotton-spinners in Lancashire.

Reels come in aluminium, in carbon fibre at 3 times the cost, and in magnesium at 6 times the cost.

(3) The Line

These are of two sorts—

(a) *Lines Which Float*

The generation of well-tweeded trout anglers fished with lines of silk rubbed with stag's grease, which is mutton fat. This oily messiness has been eradicated by nylon plastic-coated lines with a specific gravity less than 1. They are tapered at one end, and often at both, allowing the economy of reversal for longer wear. Some have fancy tapers with the weight up front, so that compleat reservoir anglers can cast as if putting the shot. Even Izaak Walton's lines were tapered, by reducing the final lengths of horsehair from seven successively down to a pair.

Floating lines are essential for dry fly-fishing, but they can be used almost as well for wet fly-fishing. At the end of the day, they generally grow dirty and soggy at the tip and sink, anyway.

(b) *Lines Which Sink*

Nylon plastic-coated lines with a specific gravity more than 1. Varying the weight varies the speed at which they sink. In some, only the tip sinks. They can be used only for wet fly-fishing.

The colours of both sorts of line serve for identification, not camouflage. It makes no difference to the fish whether the line is green, brown or white, because the fish should never see it.

As the line should comfortably fill the reel, it is attached to the centre pin by several yards of thinner line, *backing*. The backing is not meant for fishing, but its exposure in playing some enormous fish is a necessity always to be mentioned.

(4) The Cast

This is also called the *leader*.

The tweeded generation used casts of catgut,

which needed soaking to straighten them out. Now casts are of nylon filament, like surgical thread, two-and-a-half to three yards long, tapered to a fine point. Their sizes are printed on the packet in numbers, always mysteriously followed by the letter X. The higher the number the weaker the cast, because tackle makers join the fun of baffling the highly confusable incipient angler with multiple technicalities.

Incompleat anglers should equip themselves with half a dozen packets of 3 X, which has a breaking strain of five pounds. This is unlikely to be tested on a fish, but it is a reasonable strength for tugging the fly from the leaves of trees.

The same cast does for wet or dry fly-fishing, but special casts for wet flies have two *droppers*. These are short lengths knotted at right angles towards the tip, in series. A fly can be tied to each, the wet fly-fisherman thereby tripling his armament. I always cut the droppers off, because I find myself in tangles enough with one fly on the end, not three. And it is sadly not proved that increasing the target area increases the catch of fish.

The nylon filament can be bought more cheaply in reels and snipped to taste. The incompleat angler is heavy on casts. He soon finds himself amazed at the complexity of their tangles, which in their convoluted beauty can resemble the delicate Spanish silver filigree work of the eighteenth century. Even compleat anglers get themselves into tangles, which they dismiss as "wind knots". All knots weaken the cast, the nearer to the fish the more dangerously.

The ready-made casts have a loop at the near end. There is a complicated knot for creating one from the snipped length of nylon, but I just double over the thread and make a neck with a couple of simple knots, and it seems to do. The cast is attached by making a knot at the tip of the line, and linking line to loop.

I extravagantly burn last season's casts, even unused ones in their packets, if exposed to the daylight. They degenerate, and losing a good spring fish on a rotted cast causes the exquisite infuriation of self-condemnation.

Cut discarded casts into little bits, or take them home and burn them. They entangle, maim and kill birds.

(5) The Net
These are of two sorts—
(a) Ones where the net slides down the handle to resemble a basketball goal.
(b) Ones where the triangular net snaps into line with the end of its handle. These are neater to carry, but the locking device is liable to break. Unfolding them can incite anguished juggling in the incompleat angler whose rod holds his first threshing trout.

(6) The Fly
Needs its own chapter (No. 5).

Once these six items are lying on the counter, returning the gleam of their new possessor's eye, there follows *the purchase of the inessentials*.

The incipient angler will be swiftly sold some waders, though wellies will do for most fishing. And naturally a substantial plastic-lined shoulder bag to put his catch in. He will buy a green huge-pocketed waterproof jacket because he likes the look of it, and a deerstalker with the idea of decorating its peaks with flies. The shopman will smilingly present him with a little plastic box with compartments to keep his flies in, then push his luck by displaying insect repellents, wader-leak sealers, boot dryers and hand warmers (all anglers, particularly those nearing final compleation, see no need of confusing sport with discomfort). Also Swedish sheath knives, sealskin cast wallets, trays with sporting scenes and sets of cut glass decorated with the prettier variety of fly.

Warning

The incompleat angler's modest ambition to *look like* a fly-fisherman has grown more testing recently, through the reaction in many compleat anglers of trying hard not to look like anglers at all. They either don the ceremonial uniform of well-cut tweeds, beautifully-polished brogues and brown trilby hat, or they appear in patched jeans and tennis shoes and a T-shirt. Over the past twenty-five years, the deerstalker hat has, like the television set, become the badge of the masses rather than the snobs. It is better to pick the long-peaked cap worn by baseball players and golf champions, which keeps the setting sun from eyes

Admire himself in the bedroom mirror

eagerly scanning the surface for trout. But few incompleat anglers can resist a deerstalker.

Most anglers still resemble the one just out of the tackle shop. He can go home, assemble rod, reel and line, dress up in his waders and waterproof jacket, and admire himself in the bedroom mirror like a newly commissioned subaltern. From his looks, nobody could tell that he was not the most expert of fly-fishermen, and so far he has not even got his cast wet.

3
On the Trail of the Trout

3

If you want to be happy for a day, get drunk, advised the notice in the trout stream pub. *If you want to be happy for a week, get married. If you want to be happy for life, take up fishing.*

Since that yellowing wisdom behind speckled glass was first tacked to its beam, these three major diversions of mankind have defied the rigours and perils of our century to become more popular than ever, to lie within the depth of more pockets, and to be ventured upon at a progressively earlier age.

Among the many unpraised and generally unmentioned delights of our country is trout fishing always within an hour or so's drive and at a fair price.

There are four ways by which the incompleat angler, rod-tip quivering with anticipation, can make contact with his prey.

(1) Knowing Someone With Fishing

Generally impractical. A man who owns a river is soon drowned in friends.

(2) Fly-fishing Club

These abound in our clubbable land. They vary from the Houghton Club and the Piscatorial Society, which contain the compleater sort of angler, to informal associations fishing the farmers' lakes, water-filled pits and reservoirs mentioned in Chapter One. Many are not clubs at all, but a dozen or so acquaintances with the slick-sounding title of "a syndicate" combining to rent some accessible stretch of fishing. Or the landowner himself may advertise and let to all comers any number of rods — a "rod" meaning also the right of a rod to fish with his rod.

Most incipient anglers will know a fisherman from one of these institutions, who may indeed be the source of infection with the delightfully ineradicable germ. The friend will readily ask you along as his guest, gladly help you through your fumbling difficulties, patiently answer your stupid questions and wisely advise you on anything whatever to do with angling, or getting to angling, or where to stay while angling, or where to drink after angling. This is because of the—

THIRD PRINCIPLE (ALSO PLEASANT) OF INCOMPLEAT ANGLING. *An Angler in any Stage of Compleatness is Delighted Modestly to Share his Knowledge with any Less Compleat One.*

(3) Day Tickets

Even the entirely incompleat angler can find a day's fishing with no more formality nor introduction than presenting himself to buy a ticket, and a day licence, amid the beautifully polished machinery of a reservoir pumping room. Many of these reservoirs are famous, and visited eagerly by energetic anglers, who hurl their lines vast distances and come home with trout the size of duffle bags.

Chew Valley Lake on the edge of the Mendip Hills has covered with unwonted lustre the management of Bristol Waterworks. Nearby Blagdon Lake Reservoir has been entertaining fishermen lavishly since the memorably compleat G E M Skues was a springy-stepped forty. Eye Brook Reservoir by Uppingham is an attraction in the Midlands comparable to an Aston Villa cup tie, and Weir Wood spreads acres of happiness for South London commuters at East Grinstead.

These reservoirs and most others provide modestly-priced day or weekly tickets for casual fishers, though boats are extra and need booking.

In Scotland, there are ten thousand lochs and tarns all holding brown trout, and very reasonable. But under the First Principle of Scottish Angling, when a Scotsman talks of a fish he means a salmon, as when he speaks of a drink he means a whisky.

(4) Hotel Fishing

Angling is an occupation for a man on holiday soothing for both his spirit and his conscience. He *must* do it in solitude, while his wife entertains the children by taking them to visit the local ruins.

Britain is well furnished with fishing hotels. Our helpful Tourist Authority in St James's will press on you a twenty-five page roneoed list of them, with addresses, telephone numbers and rivers. The best are good enough to signal an annual visit. The others, no worse for food, comfort and obligingness than most small British provincial hotels. One pampered angler heralded his arrival at a Scottish fishing hotel with a letter enquiring if they had a private bathroom. He heard in reply that all their bathrooms were private, having bolts on the doors. Fishing hotels are always in pretty surroundings.

The British Tourist Authority's handout tells you whether the fishing is "game" (trout and salmon) or coarse (the rest), and whether it is included in the board and lodging or an extra. Some hotels have their own water (compleat anglers prefer the word "water" to specific descriptions), or have rods on water nearby. Unfortunately, the—

FOURTH PRINCIPLE OF INCOMPLEAT ANGLING states, *The Fishing at Fishing Hotels is Always Overfished.*

As the guest draws up with his family, a pair of rod clips attached to the roof of his car to show that he is a fisherman, the smiling proprietor assures him the fishing that season varies between excellent and exceptional. At the end of his guest's frustrated fortnight, the hotelier gloomily confesses himself baffled. With a tone of sympathy and self-pity, deftly indicating the misfortune to be mutual, he speculates that the water might have been too high or too low, too torrential or too sluggish, too hot or too cold. Or too coloured, he adds triumphantly ("coloured" is compleat anglers' language for muddy). Or too clear, he suggests. Or too smooth. Or too wet. Or too drumbly (even compleat anglers do not know what they mean by drumbly). He rounds off his excuses, as he prepares to shut the car door, by mentioning that his previous month's guests were planning to share the hire of a frozen food lorry for bringing home their catch.

The trout season runs from early April to late September, varying a little from one fishery to another. The best time for an angling holiday is its first three months, which brings us to the—

FIFTH PRINCIPLE OF INCOMPLEAT ANGLING. *Trout Fishing Goes Off at the Weekend of the Lord's Test Match.*

Until the end of June, from the River Kennet to the municipal waterworks, trout are liable to be hooked by wildly incompleat anglers. Afterwards, only by rather compleat ones. Perhaps this is because the summer after June becomes hotter and wetter and brighter and more thundery. Or because the trout have eaten themselves full with flies, and the fishermen have eaten themselves full with trout. Or perhaps it is because the ancient members of MCC were all devoted fishermen, and switched their pleasure from the bank to the boundary at the precise moment.

* * *

An advantage of fishing at a hotel, lost with joining a syndicate, is never again having to set eyes on any of your fellow fishers. This presents two useful opportunities—

(1) For Practice at Fishing

Hotel fishing is a pleasant practice ground for the angler to unloosen his first tangles, snag his first trees and have water first pour over the tops of his waders. Any onlooker enjoying this performance is of little consequence, because on his next year's holiday the guests will be different and the incompleat angler will — with diligence — have already accomplished his aim of *looking like a real fly-fisherman* (from a distance of not less than one hundred yards).

First trying to catch a fish, unlike first trying to play golf, has the boon of the beginner generally doing it out of sight. My own repeated swings all round a golf ball, exposed on the first tee like a spotlit solo ballet dancer, were a source of merriment to senior members of the club gazing from the bar. But even at the peak of a hotel's fishing season, when the river banks resemble a swaying bamboo fence, the angler can find some unpopular barren spot, to cast his line like a plate of spaghetti on the water in seemly secrecy.

(2) For Practice at Fishing Conversation

Another reward of learning to fish in holiday hotels is that your fellow guests are often anglers incompleat to the point of disintegration. Watch carefully for those who are *not*. Fishing hotels contain gallant and compleat anglers who catch fish with the same silent fierceness with which they descend on the vacated bathroom. (The continued popularity of trout fishing among senior officers of Her Majesty's Forces perhaps reflects the camps and airfields of Salisbury Plain and the dockyard at Portsmouth, all within reach of an evening's superb trout angling). You can quickly pick your nest of incompleat anglers in the bar, because they are the ones talking about fishing the most authoritatively.

"I tried a quickly-stripped Bloody Butcher, but with the fading light recharged my droppers with the Coachman," says one.

"Really?" sympathizes his companion with infuriating off-handedness. "Actually, I was fishing dry."

"Dry?" exclaims the other, clearly discomfited. "There wasn't much of a hatch."

"They were taking my artificial," he counters quietly.

Anguished envy seeps into the voice. "Do any good?"

"Not actually. They were coming short. How about you?"

"Not a touch all day."

"Me neither."

Comradely tranquillity is restored.

All these cost accountants, car salesmen, capstan lathe operators, marketing managers and solicitors share a desperate desire to *sound* like flyfishermen, if only when overheard. You may unscathedly learn from them how to find your way, and later hold your own, in any fishing company, if you remember three precepts—

(1) Dress Thoughtfully

You can give way to your tie with the red-and-yellow fly design *or* its matching handkerchief, but not both. And *never* a fly-patterned shirt. Not more than two dry flies may be pricked into your jacket lapel, provided they are dun coloured and never Mayflies. They are best forsworn.

(2) Stick to Skues

Enter the bar having tucked casually under your arm *The Angling Letters of G E M Skues*, or his *Minor Tactics of the Chalk Stream*, or *The Way of a Trout With a Fly*. These works have as little relevance to hotel fishing as *Moby Dick*, but G E M Skues is a useful emergency memorable name for the incompleat angler to raise the fishing conversation above the levels of his own ignorance.

Izaak Walton was the W G Grace of trout angling. Skues was the Jack Hobbs. He gazes from his frontispiece, bald, chinless, knickerbockered, paddle-handed, grasping his three-piece rod and inspecting the reader as though assessing the swiftest method of hooking him from his watery nook and banging his head on a flat stone. Skues was a Newfoundlander, a London solicitor who fished through five reigns, with particular relish on the River Itchen. He wrote for the sporting magazines, and if his prose inclines towards romantic fiction, so does Izaak Walton's. He must be forgiven a touch of all Edwardian sporting writers' weakness for florid sentences like, "Old Sol had scarce reached his zenith in the contest between the Transpontines and the Metropolitans, before the red rambler was dispatched to the outermost confines of the greensward," meaning a four in Surrey *v*. Middlesex.

Skues's work should be read as well as carried by the earnest incompleat angler. Commit to memory a short section from one of his books, or just its sub-title. For instance, *Of Generalship and the Wet Fly*, which occurs in the middle of Chapter Five in *Minor Tactics of the Chalk Stream*. Counter any downright statement by any other incompleat angler with a knowing smile and a gaze at the ceiling and, "Odd, but that's almost exactly what G E M Skues said in his remarks of generalship and the wet fly." Your propounder will fall into an uneasy silence. If he does not, he is a compleat angler, and you should rise instantly saying your wife wanted something fetching from the car.

There are many names worthy of retention by the incompleat angler, but he has enough to confuse him at the water's edge, and may well muddle the compleatly operatic H Plunket Greene with the compleatly surgical Sir Harold Gillies, who facially resembled Skues, and was the only man to catch a plaice on the fly. The great plastic surgeon was fishing for sea-trout in an estuary by night. I do not know what the plaice was doing there, but genius always attracts unusual rewards.

Stick to Skues. You will also learn something from him. The G E M was George Edward Mackenzie.

(3) Use a Limited Vocabulary

Do not utter advanced technical terms like *bulging trout* (which mean trout humping the surface like moles under the lawn) and *the presumed take* (a wild hope that you have caught one of them).

Memorize from the dialogue in Section (2) of this chapter—

A Hatch. Natural flies appearing from their larval form, or from somewhere, usually at dusk.

The Artificial. The artificial as opposed to the natural fly. Flies get the definite article and collective singular. Trout are always awarded the personal pronoun *he*.

A limited vocabulary

Do Any Good? Any success? *Did you have any luck*? is never used, compleat anglers perceiving that there is no luck whatever involved in the catching of trout.

Coming short. Playing tip-and-run.

A Touch. The fly momentarily making contact with the river bed, a piece of weed, a floating log or a fish.

Remember also—

Beat. Area of bank you are sent to patrol.

Brace. Trout are traditionally counted in twos. Five are two and a half brace. One is half a brace. This is the binary method of counting, recently adapted for use by the most advanced computers.

Cruiser. A soliciting fish.

Drag. Frightening the fish by water-skiing the dry fly.

Putting Down. Frightening the fish with your normal behaviour.

Lost. Escape of the fish through your normal clumsiness.

Foul Hooked. Fish caught anywhere but in the mouth. Uncommon, and to the more incompleat angler no foul at all.

Pricked (Got Into). See *a touch*.

A Rise. A fish revealing itself. Also used as a collective singular—"Splendid rise tonight". To the most incompleat angler, a rise is any exciting disturbance to the smooth surface of the water.

Put Back. Of no concern to the incompleat angler.

Those are sufficient terms to carry you through your early fishing evenings. You can enjoy the pleasure of eruditely discussing the day's sport with no prospect of contradiction from fellow incompleat anglers, if with no prospect of their belief either.

And if the angler *does* make a catch at his fishing hotel, even a trout the size of a handspan, he can lay it proudly on the Victorian marble washstand which is placed ceremoniously in the hall. He receives the admiration of his fellow-guests with off-hand modesty, which screens the feelings of a fast bowler inspecting a shattered stump, or a soprano a shattered glass, both emblems of exceptional human abilities and endeavour.

4
Attack

4

Casting the line is the mainspring of fly-fishing. It is a skill to be grasped before you can enjoy your new pastime, a fundamental knack like a golf swing, balancing on a bicycle, changing gear or hoisting your sails.

Casting is easier to learn than a golf swing. I know this because I once indulged in a coaching round with our pro, whom I asked in philosophic tones on the eighteenth fairway, "What do you think I *really* ought to do about my golf?" To which the poor man replied briskly, "I advise you, Doctor, to take up fishing."

SEVENTH PRINCIPLE OF INCOMPLEAT ANGLING. *A Straight Line is the Shortest Distance Between the Two Points of an Angler's Finger and a Fish's Mouth.*

Assemble your rod and reel, with its little knob sticking towards the right. Pull off three yards of line. You will strike up a mellow arpeggio of clicks, which will endure as the most evocative of music until you are a finally compleated angler.

Take the line by its knotted tip and draw it

through the rings. If you hold the rod against the ground at an angle, the line slipping from your fumbling fingers on the way will not instantly make a heap at your feet. The knot on the line will be small enough to push through the end ring of the rod. It will never go through by your waving and jiggling the rod once you have let it slip back during fishing.

Attach the nylon cast to the line, and you are ready to practise casting. Most incompleat anglers cannot resist adding their deerstalker and their Grenfell jacket and even their waders.

The tweeded generation advised casting practice on the lawn. But today's fishers are as likely to live in highrise flats, or estates with lawns barely big enough to practise the yo-yo. There seems no reason against utilizing the municipal park. Ball games may be forbidden, but these cannot include casting for non-existent fish. Anyway, THE SECOND PRINCIPLE (the Love Principle) comes into play.

Grass is no substitute for a stretch of water. Swallowing his shyness and his self-doubts, the angler must start upon his first day's fishing as soon as possible, even though handling his weapons with the dexterity of a recruit to Dad's Army.

Casting Theory
(1) *The Tackle*

In the mechanics of casting, your tackle has these properties—

(a) The fly is of insignificant weight.
(b) The three yards of nylon filament cast also are of insignificant weight.
(c) The line *has* a significant weight. Six yards of floating line pulled from the reel—the usual length, beyond the rod-tip, with which the incompleat angler first decides to torment himself—registered on my letter-balance $\frac{1}{8}$ of an ounce (3.5 grams).
(d) The rod is a spring. Its tip moves backwards and forwards about a yard. Its butt end, hardly at all. These movements are slight compared with the hurtling about of the fly which they produce above.

The combination of fly, nylon cast, line and rod is animated by the rod giving momentum to the line. Once it has started moving, the line will tug itself taut through the rings of the rod by its own weight.

Some compleatly mathematical anglers have constructed mechanical formulae for all this.

(2) *A Little Anatomy*

Casting needs two simultaneous movements.
(a) A movement at the wrist and of the wrist.
(b) A movement at the elbow *but not of* the elbow.

The wrist is a joint well designed for anglers and darts players. So is the elbow, with its hinge action (though its possibilities are more fully extended by skewering an opponent with a rapier).

But neither wrist nor elbow can be used in

isolation. Even the concert pianist playing a Chopin Nocturne is operating from the tips of his sensitive fingers to the seat of his braided pants.

The next joint up is unfortunately the shoulder. This is highly mobile and unstable, excellently designed for swimming the crawl or scratching the back of the neck, but not helpful to the angler. He must not allow the shoulder to enter actively into the movement of casting. Nor must he let the chest, the spine, the hips, the knees and the feet, as seen among some compleatly contortionist anglers. All these anatomical items are involved in the cast, but only passively. The angler must turn the rest of him into a stable platform, upon which his elbow and wrist do the work.

(3) *The Action*

Go into your living-room, taking with you a hammer and some two-inch nails. Sit yourself comfortably in a straight-backed chair, hard against the wall. Have your right elbow resting easily on the edge of a table. Pick up the hammer, and without moving your shoulder hammer a two-inch nail into the surface of the table.

Then reverse the hammer in your hand. Still keeping your elbow resting on the edge of the table, still keeping your shoulder immobile, knock another two-inch nail into the wall behind you, at the level of your head.

Once you have hammered these two-inch nails into your living-room wall and table, keep your elbow in the same place but hammer the nail behind you and the nail in front of you alternately.

It may be preferable only to pretend that you are using a hammer and nails.

You can make the same motions with an imaginary hammer, resting your elbow on the arm of your chair, or cupping it in your left hand. Get the feel of it. The nailing action is the casting action. It is a hinge movement of the elbow, accompanied by a forwards uncocking, then a backwards cocking, of the wrist. The shoulder does nothing. Transmitted to the rod, this combined movement will bring the line forwards and send it back again.

Casting a line hardly deserves to frighten the incompleat angler, who has been banging in nails all his life with no worse worry than trying to avoid hitting his thumb.

Casting in Practice

The incompleat angler will soon hear about—

(a) *The Back Cast*

The line first extends straight, from rod-tip to fly, behind the angler, horizontally, safe in the air by several feet from hooking the grass.

(b) *The Forward Cast*

The cast to catch the fish. The line doubles upon itself from the rod-tip, to assume exactly the same position in front.

RIGHT

WRONG

(c) *The False Cast*
The forward cast is not allowed to reach the water, but is flicked back again. It is the equivalent of a practice swing at golf. Repeating this movement through the air is the way to dry dry flies.

These three are really all part of the same thing—simply, the cast.

(1) The Cast, As Intended
There are four elements for the incompleat angler to carry in mind while making a cast. Even though many others—like the possibility of hooking a fish and the necessity to avoid hooking anything else—will be uppermost.

(a) *Direction*
The direction of the cast is suggested to the incompleat angler, though sadly not exactly determined for him, by the revealed or suspected position of the fish. Always remember THE SEVENTH PRINCIPLE, about keeping a straight line. A trout snaps at a fly with the speed of a camera shutter snapping a picture. If the line on the water has the swinging pattern of a fever chart, the trout will snap, but will have left before the angler can apply pressure on it to stay.

(b) *Length*
Never try to cast further than your dismally familiar limitations. It will need outstanding luck to hit the target.

(c) *Plane*

The perfect cast should be performed all in the same plane. That is, if the fly were impregnated with ink, it should trace a crisp design on a vast sheet of paper. Unfortunately, the plane of the incompleat angler's cast resembles that of the cowboy preparing to release his lasso.

The plane is important, and some of the incompleat angler's overstretched concentration should be allotted to keeping his cast moving back and forth along a fairly narrow corridor of air. This avoids catching trees and bushes both behind and before. The most infuriating of any summer's spate of angling mishaps is snagging something behind with the fly you are just about to flick forward upon the nose of an avidly rising trout. This amusingly befalls even compleat anglers, who immediately sink themselves in deeper trouble by pettishly performing numerous fancy casts to exhibit their superiority.

(d) *Delicacy*

You do not cast your fly upon the water. You cast your fly upon an imaginary surface a yard above. It then alights on the water with the delicacy of a snowflake (with the incompleat angler, more usually of a snowball).

(2) The Cast, As Performed

(a) *Holding the Rod*

Most imcompleat anglers put their thumb along the back of the handle. Freer movement flows from the thumb at the side, exactly as picking up the hammer with which you have been driving nails into your furniture.

(b) *Starting*

Apply the—

EIGHTH PRINCIPLE OF INCOMPLEAT ANGLING. *The Incompleat Angler Needs to Give Himself a Lot of Room to Do Anything.*

Obstructions behind, obstructions in front—reeds, nettles, the long grass left purposely to screen the bank—must be outdistanced. This is easier if wading is allowed.

Pull fly, nylon cast and a couple of yards of line through the ring at the end of the rod. Pull another yard off the reel. You hold this yard in your left hand, kept fairly close below your right hand. The left hand holds it back from joining in the cast, as a loop dangling under the cork handle of the rod.

Some experts advise your right foot forward. Others, your left. Anyway, make sure that you stand feeling comfy.

Waggle the rod perpendicularly, appreciating its springy action.

Now we come to the difficult bit.

Flick the line beind you, with your hammering motion. There is your back cast. When the line is—or should be—fully extended horizontally, flick it into your forward cast, again with the hammering movement. Repeat. You are false casting, even if the line is swishing round the peaks of your deerstalker.

Suddenly you feel the line come to life. It moves! All on its own! But the rod is moving hardly at all—just its yard forward and yard back, always stopping (in the hands of the compleat angler) at the perpendicular.

The compleat angler's cast has the velvety acceleration and deceleration of a Rolls-Royce. Remember that a smooth action in the air means a straight line on the water. And a fly brought to an abrupt halt will fly off for ever.

The cast is created by the controlled stopping and re-starting of the rod, in its narrow movement back and forward. The incompleat angler must keep his rod stationary just long enough for the line to roll out over the rod-tip, straight and horizontal, before starting it off again in exactly the opposite direction. He might indeed ask for how long he must make this essential pause.

"Might I indeed ask for how long must I make this essential pause? Particularly with the back cast, when I am looking straight ahead. I do have to look straight ahead all the time, don't I?"

"Glancing over the shoulder while casting is the mark of the incorrigibly incompleat angler, just as taking the eye off the ball distinguishes the eternally hopeless golfer."

"That was pompous."

"Sorry."

"Well, tell me. Exactly how long must I keep the rod still for these two pauses?"

"It's all a matter of experience."

"May I say that's a rather stupid reply?"

WRONG

WRONG
Glancing over the shoulder

"Perhaps it is. But there's no other."
"That was a bit pompous, too."
"Kindly leave the page."

(c) *Fishing*

Get the hang of false casting. It works up confidence. After an hour or so you should achieve your first object of looking like a fly-fisherman, if glimpsed briefly through the bushes.

Then you decide excitedly to fire at a fish.

The incompleat angler finishes his false cast forwards, and follows through powerfully with his rod to push the fly upon the water —or even, if he remembers, its imaginary surface a yard above. This has the effect upon the fish of a tree trunk dropping in lengthways.

You do not *push* your fly on the water. *No more force is needed on the rod for a real cast than for a false cast.*

You bring the rod to its usual halt about a yard in front of the perpendicular. Now you come to the only difference between a false cast and a fighting cast. You *shoot line*.

Release the slack held below the cork handle in your left hand. This will be drawn forward by the weight of the already airborne line. The extra yard of line—which can grow in length as you grow in compleatness—streaks out towards the fish, without needing previously to be waved about the countryside, when it has every chance of hooking a piece of it.

Shooting the line allows the fly to fall upon the

water with naturalistic gentleness. The rod now continues to move forwards. *You* do not move it. *The line* moves it. You can slacken your grip, and let the rod follow the line passively. Your only action is to stop it when the fly touches down. Otherwise, the rod will fall into the water.

Compleat anglers will demonstrate to you this shooting the line. They will show how they let rod follow line, by holding the cork handle for its final descent in the open palm.

If the incompleat angler keeps his mind fixed throughout his casting—back cast or forward cast, false cast or true—that it is all going to end by his stopping the rod in its normal forward position, then letting rod follow shot line effortlessly, he has cleared his way throught the thickets of confusion with which casting is overgrown.

You may complain that this chapter is confusing enough in itself.

"May I complain that this chapter is confusing enough?"

"Yes, but I obviously had to have one on casting. The only way you can remotely understand what I'm getting at is taking your rod and going down to the river bank and fiddling about."

"I wish you'd put that at the beginning."

The incompleat angler—should he not have caught his fish—pulls in most of his line with his left hand, *lifts* the rest off the water, and starts casting again.

(3) Complications

(a) *Wind*

Instruction manuals on casting place the incompleat angler in the same climatic conditions as the Ancient Mariner. There is nearly always wind on water. You should utilize it, trying to ensure it blows behind you, to carry your line out forwards. This is contrived easily when fishing on a lake from a boat. When you are learning to cast, start with the wind behind you even if there is no possibility of fish in front.

If the wind is blowing in your face, then you are permitted to add force to the final descent of the rod. When your shot line runs forward under its own momentum, bring the rod-tip down an extra yard sharply. This should force your line through the wind.

You will get the feel of this movement only with practice, like the feel of casting against a cross-wind. All really compleat anglers can cast as accurately as usual whichever way the wind is blowing, though they sensibly respond to a howling gale in their faces by making for the nearest pub with a log fire, like the rest of us.

(b) *Snags*

If you are snagged, lay your rod on the ground, taking care not to tread on it in your irritation. Grasp the line beyond the rod-tip in both hands, and pull against the obstruction steadily. Either the fly will tear out, or you will snap the cast. In either event, the problem is solved.

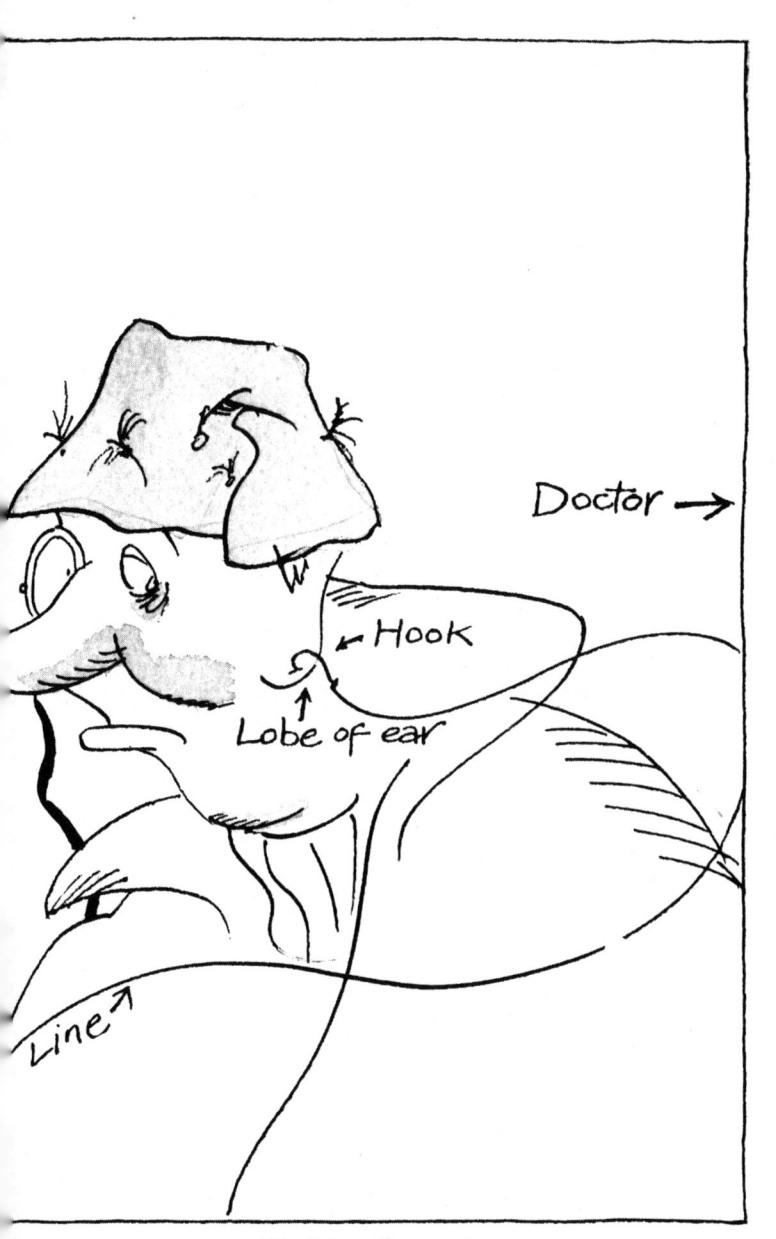

The lobe of your ear

If you hook the lobe of your ear, snip off the cast and seek a doctor. It is impossible to push the barb out again without a painful and disproportionate wound. The treatment is to push the barb on through the unbroken skin, then clip it off with wire-cutters. Practitioners in fishing areas keep a pair of these handy. The operation is performed with a dose of local anaesthetic.

(c) *Fancy Casts*

The vast space of reservoirs incites their anglers to enormously long casts. The "Double Line Haul" is a fearsome new name for a cast used over the years by competitive anglers to win silver cups at game fairs.

As the rod gets into its stride bending backwards, the expert hauls yards of line from it with his left fist. When the rod approaches the end of its backward journey, he lets the line go again. He repeats the whole trick as the rod bends forwards. By this method he can cast nonchalantly across a football pitch from touchline to touchline, if not goalmouth to goalmouth.

We incompleat anglers can find ourselves in trouble enough trying to catch trout a dozen yards from our own feet. Besides, the double line haul is terribly tiring.

The Spey Cast, the Wye Cast, the Steeple Cast and all others are best excluded from the incompleat angler's ambitions and even conversation.

(d) *Boats*

Fishing on a lake or reservoir may have you

casting sitting in a boat. This does not complicate the basic principles. It needs the same movement to cast sitting down as to cast standing up, which will probably tip you in the water. If you are sharing a boat, be clear about the order and the direction in which you are each going to cast. Two incompleat anglers casting at the same moment from both ends of the same boat may take some hours to untangle.

Even when there are no fish in sight, or if the river has been poached empty, the incompleat angler must cast all the time he finds himself with some water, for practice. Accuracy of casting is of first importance in angling. The fruitfulness of all angling techniques derives from it. Erudite anglers dazzle us with books on their relentless ways of catching fish, but they are perhaps hiding with unwitting modesty a dexterity which would trap a trout with a bare bent pin.

5
The Great Deception

5

Flies compose a subject even more confusing for the incompleat angler than casting. There are many books about them, which are more confusing still. Neither obstacle is of much significance. It does not matter to the incompleat angler if he knows nothing about flies at all.

The confusion arose from the Victorians' enthusiasm over the classification of all creatures great and small. This was the fall-out of the biological bombshell dropped on them by Charles Darwin, *On the Origin of Species* in 1859. The busily painstaking science of taxonomy classified all things, from wise and wonderful man via the chimpanzees down to sponges and the single-celled amoeba. They were split into huge groups, which were partitioned into smaller classes, then into orders and next into families. The families were further divided into genera, and the genera into species.

Any humble being, inoffensively making its way through its world—a sea squirt, perhaps, a koala bear, a tapeworm, a newt—could no longer lose itself in the isolation of individualism. It became a clearly labelled, instantly placeable—if negligibly important—part of a cleverly ordered scheme of things which was created by beings of far higher intelligence than itself. It is exactly the same with the present-day British public and the Civil Service.

The turn of all things bright and beautiful for earnest classification came towards the end of the nineteenth century. Eager amateur naturalists pranced through lush and fragrant summer fields, joyful with butterfly-net and hand-lens, and many of them in Holy Orders. They fell upon the flies and sorted them out.

Every fly which flutters through a fisherman's environment is readily recognized by the entomologist under its scientific name. These names are adapted from Latin and Greek. An entomologist who speaks only Cantonese Chinese and another fluent solely in the Pushtu dialect of Afghanistan may thus understand what each is speaking about. But the fisherman cannot. He recognizes the fly as accurately as the scientists, but he gives it another name. He may also give this name to other flies which the entomologist insists are entirely different ones. The fisherman uses different names from the scientist for the different stages of development of the fly. And when he buys an imitation fly to catch his fish, the tackle-maker has yet another name for it.

If dogs suffered an existence at such cross-purposes as flies, the long-eared, short-legged specimen waddling down the street would be recognized by the zoologist as *Canis familiaris*. To the fond owner, it is a basset hound. But this owner might for his own convenience include under basset hounds both beagles and cocker spaniels, and mention in conversation that they had grown from lovely kittens. And if the dog owner wanted to buy an imitation stuffed basset hound for his daughter, he would have to ask the shopman for something like a Cruft's Fancy.

Sources of Confusion—1

A Little Entomology

The fly starts, like the rest of us, from a fertilized egg. The egg turns into a larva. The larvae of some creatures are familiar from our childhood—the caterpillar which grows into a butterfly, the tadpole which becomes a frog. The larva is a useful biological gimmick. Being different from the adult, it can explore and exploit a different environment to achieve its maturity.

The larvae of the flies which excite fish and fisherman live under water. Their anatomy is simple. They nourish themselves on algae and mosses, fragments of plants and other larvae. They breathe by diffusing oxygen from the water. They crawl or swim about. The compleatly entomological angler recognizes stages in their development until they are fully grown and sturdy. As their skin can expand no more than the angler's trousers, when they fatten they have repeatedly to discard it. With their final moult, they split the larval covering and emerge on the water's surface as an adult, called the *imago*. This is metamorphosis, the change from grub to beauty, the plot for Cinderella.

Caddis flies, the alder fly, and other insects like butterflies have an extra stage between the larva and the adult, the *pupa* or chrysalis. Neither feeding nor moving, the pupa appears as lifeless as an Egyptian mummy. But inside, the body is reorganizing itself and nourishing upon itself, until the pupa floats to the surface and splits to emit its adult.

The Ephemeroptera—"mayflies" in their correct and widest definition—do not spring into the world fully adult from the larva. An immature fly first appears, called the *subimago*. This is dull-coloured, its wings covered with fine hairs. It flutters with the breeze to a sheltering riverside leaf, to moult again within the hour and take to the air as the final version, the imago.

The life of the imago is short but delightful, being wholly occupied with sex. The males swarm over the water, grabbing any female in sight and enjoying her in mid-air. The female lays her eggs upon the water and floats away in post-coital exhaustion.

The fisherman calls the dull-coloured, hair-covered subimago a dun. He calls the fully adult imago a spinner. The moribund mother he dismisses as a spent gnat.

To summarize—

Form	Scientific Word	Angler's Word
Between egg and adult	Larva Pupa	Nymph
Immature adult	Subimago	Dun
Mature adult	Imago	Spinner
Dying female adult	—	Spent Gnat

Sources of Confusion—2

The trout has an interest in four classes of flies.
(1) *Ephemeroptera*, the mayflies.
(2) *Plecoptera*, the stoneflies.
(3) *Trichoptera*, the caddis flies.
(4) Oddments like *Sialis lutaria* the alder fly, and *Bibio johannis* the black gnat.
The most numerous and important of these are (1).

Mayflies do not appear only in May, but all through the summer. And when an angler speaks of a mayfly he means a particular sort of mayfly, the *Ephemera danica*. This is an enormous fly, which descends on "mayfly rivers" like the Kennet for a short season towards midsummer—not in May, which would be less confusing, but in early June.

It compares to the humdrum fly population as a swarm of Jumbos among light aircraft. The trout grow recklessly greedy for this abundant meal of huge portions, and the syndicates of fishermen have rules barring guests during the period, so that they may thoroughly enjoy the slaughter. To these compleat anglers, this time is called simply "The Mayfly". It is also known as "Duffers' Fortnight".

The mayfly angler names the big mayfly dun the Green Drake. He does not call the mayfly female spinner the Green Duck, but the Grey Drake. The other mayflies which flit their unobtrusive way through the rest of the season he does not call mayflies at all. During the last century they were given names like Claret Duns and Sherry Spinners, which with Large Dark Olives and even Pale Wateries suggest that the Victorian anglers were a convivial lot.

To summarize—

Names of Common Flies

Scientific Words	Angler's Words
Ephemeroptera	Flies
These *Ephemeroptera* include—	
Ephemera danica	Mayfly
Leptophlebia vespertina	Claret Dun, Claret Spinner
Ephemerella ignita	Blue-winged Olive Dun, Sherry Spinner
Baëtis bioculatus (and others)	Pale Watery
Baëtis scambus (and others)	Olive Dun
Baëtus pumilus (and others)	Iron Blue (This is supposed to be the only fly which has a taste to

	trout, though God knows
	how anyone found out)
Baëtis rhodani	Olive Dun, Red Spinner
Rhithrogena haarupi	March Brown
Caenis macrura	Fisherman's Curse

Another order—
Plecoptera   Stoneflies

Another—
Trichoptera   Caddis Flies
These *Trichoptera* include—
Halesus radiatus   Caperer
Sericostoma personatum Welshman's Button
Mystacidea longicornis Silverhorns
Brachycentrus subnubilus Grannom

The *Chironomidae* are non-biting midges, called by anglers Blae and Black, or Buzzers.

You may think this list too comprehensive for the incompleat angler.

"I think this list is too comprehensive. How can I possibly remember that lot? I can't even understand it. It reads to me like a list of rather nasty diseases."

"You don't need to remember a word. You didn't even have to read it. I put it in for reference. Though if you can retain one or two of those Latin names, it's awfully impressive in conversation with other incompleat anglers."

"But what if I want to buy some flies? I've got to do that before I can even start."

Victorian anglers were a convivial lot

"Use the fancy names they're sold under, like all other anglers, even the compleatly puristic ones."

There are also plenty of biting midges about river banks. On warm evenings, it is worth the angler smearing himself with insect repellent.

* * *

Buying Flies

The incompleat angler's selection should be guided by—
(1) *Size*
(2) *Colour*
(3) *Shopman's Advice*

First, he must be clear whether he is going wet fly-fishing or dry fly-fishing. *Wet flies* are made to be fished under the surface of the water, deceiving the trout by representing nymphs, beetles, freshwater shrimps, peamussels, bristle worms, caterpillars, small fish, woodlice, fragments of sandwich or anything else which is edible and moving. Trout have been known even to eat a mouse. They eat more things coming from the bottom of the river than from the top, so the angler starting on wet fly-fishing can play himself in on an easier wicket.

Artificial flies are made from bits of fur, feather and nylon thread, often dyed and— with wet flies — often brightened with a twist of tinsel. Of the vast computations of colours which the shop can offer their customers, the incompleat angler should start with a selection of six. Trout have the same types of cell in their eyes as we have, and are not colour blind. (And neither are flies.)

Predominant Colour	Fancy Name
Red	Bloody Butcher
Yellow	Invicta
Brown	March Brown
Green	Teal and Green
Blue	Teal and Blue
Black and White	Coachman

Buy medium size, always at least two of each variety, in case you excitedly snag a proved effective deceiver in a tree.

Ask the shopman's advice, in return for which you must allow him to sell you some flashy flies like the Alexandra or Black and Peacock Spider.

Only the more venturesome angler starts his angling with a *dry fly*. Unlike wet flies, these bristle with hackles, which keep them afloat. They can imitate only a fly. Not a nymph, or a pea-mussel, or a caterpillar or a piece of sandwich.

A selection made on the same principles would produce —

Predominant Colour	Fancy Name
Red	Red Tag
Yellow	Greenwell's Glory
Brown	March Brown
Green	An Olive
Blue	Iron Blue
Black and White	Black Gnat

Ask the shopman's advice, and let him sell you a Tup's Indispensable.

Artificial *nymphs* are bought by dry fly-fishermen to imitate larvae as they float to the surface before bursting into subimagos, the duns of summer-long mayflies. As nymphs are presented to the trout under water, there is no reason why nymphs, too, should not deceive the trout with the appearance of passing pea-mussels, bristle worms, freshwater shrimps, woodlice or bits of bully beef.

Shop nymphs have rudimentary hackles and no wings, and looking rather uninteresting are not purchased by incompleat anglers. It is worth buying a yellow nymph—known under the confusion principle as an amber nymph—a grey nymph, the famous pheasant tail nymph and a nymph called a Green Chomper, which is seemingly made from billiard cloth and can bring disproportionate reward to the incompleatest angler.

Some compleatly dexterous anglers tie their own flies. Catching a trout on your home-made fly is said to give the profound satisfaction of motherhood, or of holing in one.

The fly itself is attached to the line by the *Incompleat Angler's Knot*. This is the only knot he need ever learn.

Hold the fly firmly between the tips of thumb and forefinger of the left hand. Push two inches of the nylon cast (two inches is excessive, but remember the EIGHTH PRINCIPLE, about giving yourself plenty of room) through the eye of the fly. Grip securely the U of cast in the eye of the fly, with the finger-tips holding the fly.

The Gordonian Knot

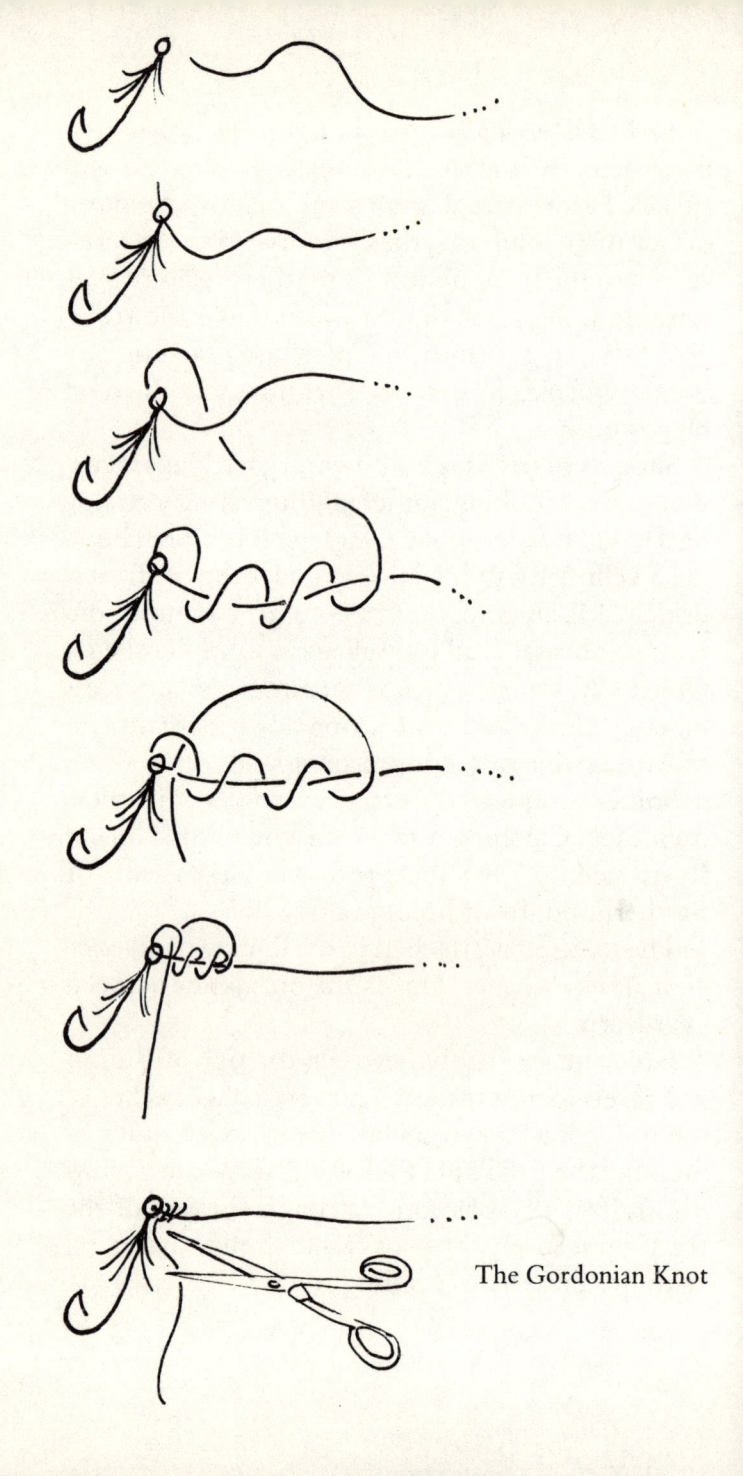

With the tips of the right thumb and forefinger, wind the spare two inches round the main length of the cast. Be sure you leave a generous loop before making the first twist. Dig the end which is still free — after making these three twists — through this loop. Add this free end to the grip between your left thumb and index finger, in which you are already holding the fly and the U of the cast. Steadily pull the main length of the cast, to tighten everything up. This is a half-blood knot, named after a Dr Blood. It has no surgical application, and the doctor did not invent it, but cunningly X-rayed his way into a tackle-maker's secrets.

You snip the free end down to a quarter of an inch with the pair of fine pointed scissors borrowed from your wife's sewing things. If you have already lost them, use your teeth. You should also borrow a pin from your wife. It is essential for picking out bits of old cast blocking fly-eyes. And a sewing-machine needle, if available. This is exactly the right shape for opening up the knots most often made in the cast, the involuntary ones.

Steady pressure will drive a pin-point through an apparently solid blob of tightly knotted nylon. A sewing machine needle then creates a loop which will slide off the flangeless head. The loosening may be effortlessly completed by following up the sewing-machine needle with a plastic golf-tee. This sequence is my only original contribution to angling technique. It is the area in which I have enjoyed the greatest experience.

* * *

Anglers in all stages of compleation share continually the same problem— *What Shall I Tie On?*

Its answer is the — NINTH PRINCIPLE OF INCOMPLEAT ANGLING. *Pick Your Fly by Asking Someone Who Knows the Water.*

Local experience and local information are the surest arguments to draw fingers towards a particular fly in the box. Dry fly-anglers, all of whom are compleat, conscientiously imitate the fly which they see on the water, or ought to see on the water. If the medium olive dun is rising from the surface, they tie on their Gold-ribbed Hare's Ear. If they notice the red spinner falling back again, they apply their Lunn's Particular. Such sophistication is beyond the incompleat angler. But he should not feel downhearted. Because a hungry trout will eat more or less anything.

The monstrous eight-pounder, fattened in its stewpond like a prize sow on reddish-coloured trout pellets of horsemeat, is slipped into the most expensive of trout streams to be triumphantly hooked by an oil sheikh, on his first cast with his recommended reddish fly. Then some summer evenings, the river is aboil with rising fish, but they are eating a microscopical fly and spurn the compleatest anglers' confections.

In wet fly-fishing it does not matter too much what fly you have on. Though after half an hour or so, an unsuccessful colour can be changed for

Hooked by an oil sheikh

another. This encourages the fisherman, if not the fish. During the mayfly season, I have caught trout with the floating plastic grasshopper, from the Ginza in Tokyo. One angler on the Itchen, the river sanctified by Walton and Skues, tied on a brownish fly at the start of the season and untied it at the end, and caught as many trout as anyone.

The water-meadows at the end of World War Two were bright with buttercups and abuzz with flies. Today they are dull and silent. The pesticides have killed the insects, the herbicides have killed the wild flowers, the chain saws have culled the bushes and trees. The swarming hatches of fly have gone for ever. When flies are sparse the trout will take what is going, rather than a particular sort. The dry fly-fisherman's doctrine of imitating the fly on the water has been diluted. Flies are becoming of less importance in fly-fishing, a paradox as sad for the incompleat as for the most expertly compleat angler.

6
The Artless Dodger

6

There are two sorts of trout.

(1) Brown Trout

Salmo trutta. A native fish of the British Isles, of Europe to the southern slopes of the Pyrenees, of Asia as far west as the Urals and the Aral Sea, of North Africa in the Atlas Mountains.

But the Empire Builders, with their enormous greenheart rods, saw no reason why distance from home should deprive them of their trout fishing, no more than of their Keatings Insect Powder and traditional Christmas, all of which they transported with them. The descendants of both the men and the fish continue the sport today in the Veldt of South Africa, between Melbourne and Sydney and in Tasmania, in Kenya, and in the compleatly angling country of New Zealand. Also in southern Chile, Vancouver and New England.

"Brownies" are pretty fish. They have dark backs, golden bellies and a line of haloed spots both brown and red running from eye to tail.

Their colour varies with the season and the water. The pigment cells of a trout's skin respond to the eye, and the fish behave as sluggishly-reacting underwater chameleons. A diseased trout with its pigment control lost turns an ugly, blotchy, greyish black colour.

Though brown trout breed naturally in British waters, many of those caught have been fathered by the fish farmer.

(2) Rainbow Trout

Salmo gairdnerii. The Americans returned the Empire Builders' compliment by bringing the rainbow trout to Britain in 1882 from the Sacramento River of California. Rainbows have followed the brown trout round the world, and in New Zealand grow enormous.

Rainbows do not breed easily in British waters. But they are more popular products of the fish hatcheries than brownies. They survive with higher temperatures and less oxygen than brown trout, common conditions in the many shallow, sluggish lakes which incompleat anglers enjoy. Rainbows grow faster, but live not so long.

Rainbows are flashing, silvery fish, with a closely-speckled red band down each side. The golden-bellied brownie is more dignified. Though reluctant to be pulled towards its end by an angler's line, it never threshes all over the surface of the water. The rainbow, once hooked, generally becomes airborne.

A dozen varieties of trout were once described

in Britain, but since the beginning of the century they were recognized as local variations. All trout are trout, even sea trout. The steelhead trout *(Salmo gairdnerii gairdnerii)* is a form of rainbow from the Pacific coast of America, sometimes added to English fisheries for variety. The fontanalis trout *(Salvelinus fontinalis),* also called the brook trout and the speckled trout, a native of New England which occasionally diverts British anglers, is a char. These names prove that the conspiracy to confuse incompleat anglers is an international one.

The grayling *(Thymallus thymallus)* is a companion of the trout where the streams descend between hills rather than mountains. They are fish with soft mouths and large dorsal fins, which come to the fly and make tasty treats for the cat. There are no grayling in Ireland.

* * *

You can catch trout by dragging a long net through the water. Or passing across it an electric current. Or chucking in a stick of gelignite. Poaching— which is stealing fish— and vandalism have become almost as common today in trout fisheries as in the rest of the country.

But the sport of angling is an expression of self-discipline. That is why an angler at any stage of compleation is a man who can control his passions. Anglers are all steady husbands and drivers, sober and without overdrafts, and never leave litter. They are peaceable men. Mr Neville

Hitler was not.

Chamberlain was a trout fisherman. Hitler was not.

The ways in which anglers have decided that fish should be caught — wet fly, dry fly and nymphing — each have their own simple regulations. Wet fly-fishing has the simplest.

Rivers or lakes (including reservoirs) can be fished with both wet and dry fly and even nymph, but the incompleat angler will probably start his career fishing wet fly on some artificial sheet of water.

He finds himself in decent solitude on the bank. He is fully uniformed in waders and deerstalker, fishing bag slung in exciting anticipation across his shoulders. He has arrived untorn by barbed wire and ungored by bulls (there is no such animal as a reliable bull, whatever the farmers like to tell you). Perhaps he has stumbled upon a "hot spot", the bankside grass trampled flat by a herd of knowing anglers.

With luck, the day is overcast, the wind from the south-west. Izaak Walton wished the honest angler that the east wind may never blow when he goes a-fishing, and its effect has not changed in the slightest over three and a quarter centuries. Accurately foretelling the next few hours' weather is essential to the angler. There are many complex portents which he can learn to interpret in the skies, but I find it less trouble listening to the reliable forecasts on the BBC.

The angler holds his new rod, a Bloody Butcher securely attached to its cast, its hook pricked into the cork handle, the cast itself looped round the reel, the line taut. Remembering the EIGHTH PRINCIPLE (allowing a lot of room), he achieves an immediate hinterland free of trees, bushes and barbed-wire fences. He is confident he knows all about casting. He detaches his fly, pulls three yards of line through the ring at the end of his rod, and searches the surface with eyes gleaming like a bride on her wedding morn.

He *looks* as compleat as any angler. What does he do next?

* * *

A Little Zoology

The trout is a ridiculously stupid creature.

Its brain is sandwiched between its eyeballs. This is the size of a split pea in the tasty little wild trout to be caught in the tumbling rock-strewn streams of Scotland and South Wales. It is no bigger than a kidney bean in the inedible monstrosities reared on fish pellets in Hampshire stewponds. The brain never grew larger than a walnut in those grotesque trout inside the glass cases of fishing hotels — but these were pet fish, fondly fed until they died a natural death, when their owners would have no more considered consuming them than roasting and eating the dog.

The front portion of a trout's brain is concerned with nothing but smelling. The middle, the largest bit, only with seeing. The rear part is a combination of gyroscope and boiler-clock, controlling balance and movement, and the functions of bodily housekeeping.

The trout's sight is the sense of most importance to itself and to the man who is trying to catch it. The optic lobe of its brain is served by a pair of eyes which look sideways. These eyes work much like a man's. Trout are short-sighted.

The trout's window on the world is like a circular skylight, glazed with a lens which focuses a fairly wide area into the pair of sideways-looking eyes. The window's images are distorted — the fly on the surface looks vastly nearer than the incompleat angler himself who has managed to plonk it there from five yards away.

Outside this circular skylight, the bed of the lake is reflected back again. The picture is roughly like looking through a hole in the Hall of Mirrors. But the underwater world is dim. And increasing ripples on the surface have the effect of thickening fog upon the human eye.

Trout do not see much dead ahead. But they can hold their position in a current by fixing their gaze on some object and keeping it there, as a sailor shifts his body to hold the horizon level in his eyes. The trout's eyes find its food. They are particularly attracted by the *movement* of anything to eat. They can shift their eyes in their sockets a little, but having no eyelids cannot close them. Nobody can tell if a trout is asleep or awake. It does not know itself.

The ears of the trout, like those of the angler, are involved in keeping balance. The trout has no earholes letting upon the outside world, but it can distinguish sounds. More important to the fish are the vibrations picked up from the pair of "lateral lines" running along its body. These can sense even the movement of another fish. The thudding and sploshing of incompleat anglers comes through like a passing liner on a submarine's asdic.

Trout smell and taste. A Canadian ichthyologist says that fish smell as well as any land animal—and that human saliva attracts them. So to outwit his prey, the incompleat angler will choose a patch of ripple, approach stealthily, stay outside the trout's window, and keep his fly on the move in the water, after having spat on it lavishly for luck.

The trout has no memory and no reasoning. It has no passions, no imagination. It is aware only of being alive, often hungry and fancying a bit of sex in the winter.

The Lord of Creation has a brain like a pair of cauliflowers. Biologists have removed the whole front two-thirds of a trout's brain, depriving it of smell and sight. It swims about as busily as before. Remove the frontal bits of a man's brain, and he will shortly be in serious trouble with the police.

After three and a half hundred million years of separation there are still similarities between the beings on one end of the rod and the other. In good condition, both can see well and move quickly. If they are really hungry, they will seize anything edible in sight. If they are sated, food does not interest them, however appetising. If they are scared, they lie low. If the weather is bad, they prefer not to move at all. Thunder frightens them. Once either has suffered a brush with death on its daily travels, it proceeds on its way with new-found caution. Each knows its own home, and likes to stay near it.

If the incompleat angler recognizes the behaviour which he shares with the trout, it will arm him to catch one.

Trout are often larded with flattery by the romantic books. The fish is imbued with such wiliness and cleverness, such retentiveness and logic, such observation and intuition, that the angler would seem to be setting out each morning to bring home a bag of Sherlock Holmeses.

To flatter the trout with brains is really to flatter the fisherman. Repeatedly baffled and saddened by the failure of his little plots and traps, the Lord of Creation finds it more comfortable to imagine that the trout has outwitted him, rather than evaded him by the simple reflexes which the Lord of Creation started to abandon when their common ancestor crawled up the waterless bank on its fins.

But it is sadly familiar knowledge to the angler that trout become "educated". They grow wary and immune to the compleatest tricks.

Inhibiting reflexes can be instilled in fish as in other beings. There was this pike in a tank, which banged its nose on the glass partitioning it from some edible fish, and learned painfully to leave them alone even when the transparent division was removed. And this octopus, which never tried to eat the tempting crab after the biologist spiced it with an electric shock.

These experiments may be performed more simply by casting a fly at a trout and failing to hook it. All beings from primitive flat-worms up to men learn by trial and error — that is, the hard way. In the trout, the anti-fly reflex cannot remain imprinted upon its brain for long, unless renewed — but in heavily fished water it is, daily, even hourly.

Trout discover like any other creatures to distinguish what is edible and what is not. The art of angling is presenting a lure that looks like food and moves like food. The care, skill, ingenuity and experience needed to achieve this perfectly with the fly are beyond the incompleat angler. But he can take heart that a trout when hungry is inclined to be careless. And that luck can favour both ends of the rod.

7
Catching Your Fish

7

The incompleat angler, gazing with fervid expectation over the water, may classify his prey into—
(1) *Trout Revealed*
(2) *Trout Suspected*
(3) *Trout Wildly Hoped For*

(1) Trout reveal themselves by breaking or disturbing the surface of the water after food. They do this in four ways.
(a) They silently make a ring, sucking down a fly emerging from the nymph.
(b) They come partly out of the water and return, making a plop.
(c) They take an insect just under the surface of the water, showing their backs like sportive porpoises.
(d) They do not show themselves at all, but simply ripple the surface.

The incompleat angler, like the medical student, must learn to appreciate that there is *some* abnormality before his eyes, and to interpret it.

Rainbow trout in hot weather may reveal

themselves dramatically by leaping several feet in the air. This is the equivalent of the perspiring angler throwing off his jacket, and unlikely to lead to their capture. But it is worth a cast or two. To the incompleat angler, *anything* within range is worth a cast or two.

Movements other than fish can ruffle the surface. Trout swimming shallowly make a V "bow wave", which is really a wake. This revelation, too, is unlikely to create a catch. But it is again worth having a try.

Swallows swooping for flies make rings on the water like their competitors the trout. Voles and grass snakes sometimes excite the fisherman. Methane bubbles up from below — "The bottom of the loch farting, soor," to the Irish gillie. A breeze ruffling the surface demands a sharp eye to discern the movement of trout just beneath.

The trout can be seen below the water, particularly with polaroid glasses. These are a necessity for dry fly-fishermen, who appear on the banks during bright afternoons like an outing of the Mafia. The trout can also see the fisherman. Approach stealthily, from downstream, which is behind the stationary trout's tail. Once the trout sees or senses the angler, it is off like a sprinter from the gun.

Move about the river bank, and wade along the river bed, with a gentle, deliberative step, as though fearful of waking a loud-lunged baby. When moving along the water and not fishing, keep well clear of the bank. You *should* move, all through the day. If there are no fish in sight, go and look for some. Angling is not a passive sport. Do not confuse patience with laziness.

(2) The suspicion of a trout's presence is most fruitfully formed from the angler's experience of the water.

The fisherman often finds himself staring across a river or lake which is shimmering unbrokenly in the sunshine. He can prowl about, hoping with his natural forbearance that trout will show itself. Or he can attack where he suspects that a trout might be lying. Trout are home-loving creatures. They find a pleasant patch and they stay there, even as little fry. Of second importance in angling, after accuracy in casting, is knowing the location of your fish as thoroughly as the names, addresses and telephone numbers of your friends.

The angler's first suspicions proving unfounded, he chances his fly in the little backwaters, or the eddies round rocks and between the piers of bridges, or in the froth-speckled calm beyond the torrent formed by sluices ("hatches" to compleat anglers). Or anywhere he imagines that a trout could lie comfortably in the calm while waiting for the faster water to serve it with food. Trees are worth fishing under, because insects drop from them. It needs a fair degree of completion for the angler to shoot his line under the low branches instead of right into them.

Angling without a target is known as "Fishing

the Water", an elegant way of saying trying your luck.

(3) The wild hope of trout is all that sustains the angler on days when a blazing sun has burnt all opposition from the sky, or when the air is heavy with thunder growling round the horizon, or the rain is coming down in curtains. Even compleat anglers shake their heads and go home to watch television.

If the incompleat angler is fishing wet fly, and has a line manufactured to sink, he can cast as far as possible, and wait as long as possible, and retrieve it as slowly as possible from the deep. Otherwise, he can sit in his car and read a paperback until the sun sets, the thunder clears away or the rain stops. The wait will be worth while, because trout celebrate their release from all three trying conditions with a rewarding friskiness.

* * *

The incompleat angler sets about capturing the fish, either discerned or suspected, by one of the traditional methods permitted him. These vary with the water. They were first enumerated in Chapter Two as—
(1) Wet Fly
(2) Dry Fly
(3) Nymphing

There is another useful method not mentioned in angling instruction manuals—
(4) Damp Fly

(1) The wet fly method is described as, "Chuck it and chance it" — fairly justifiably, too. As the form of angling embodying the greatest proportion of luck, it must recommend itself to the incompleat angler.

Wet fly-fishing is allowed on most lakes and reservoirs. When you see a trout moving (the comprehensive word used by compleat anglers for rings, bulges and all forms of trout activity), approach stealthily and cast your wet fly in the middle of it. Remember the SEVENTH PRINCIPLE, and keep your line straight. This is easy to achieve in wet fly-fishing, because once the cast is made, your left hand draws the line back through the water, attracting the fish by moving the fly. It has the bonus of immediately straightening out a line which falls into the water like a bundle of knitting.

The cast will not be wasted if it fails to hit the centre of the ring made by a rising trout. The disturbance to the water announces that the trout is about, and feeding. As your fly passes its vision, it will turn and snap at it.

Or perhaps not.

On a river, wet fly-fishing can be done upstream or downstream. The incompleat angler can let his line be carried down by the current, and retrieve it with confidence in its straightness. Casting upstream, he has to gather his line in briskly before it becomes wound round his waders.

Retrieving the line is straightforward. Hold it

with your right forefinger against the cork handle of the rod. With your left thumb and forefinger, just below your right hand, pull it steadily in. Twining it neatly round your fingers is an unnecessary complication. Let it drop untidily on the bank or the bottom of your boat. The pace of retrieving the line can be varied from snail to squirrel, but this does not make much difference to your chances.

Fish are caught with the wet fly mostly where the fly lands, but they are liable to take the fly at any time in its passage back to the rod. The "take" may sometimes be almost unnoticeably gentle. If you are using a sinking line, watch for a change in the angle it seems to make entering the water.

Wet flies are used for salmon fishing, which is done mostly in Scotland and Ireland by Americans. Everything is on a grander scale than with trout — two-handed rod, reels as big as saucers, vivid flies with frightening names like Thunder and Lightning, Bloody Mary and Black Doctor, chestwaders, attendant gillies, vast fees.

Another salmon method uses a short rod and multiplying reel to drag a shiny lump of metal repeatedly through the water, in the touching state of mind which puts pools coupons in the post week after week for a lifetime. The average rod-hours to catch a salmon have been worked out by ichthyologists, and run from 7.8 right up to 86 hours. After half a week of solid angling, even the most incompleat trout man would have caught a light breakfast.

(2) Dry fly-fishing is done only by compleat anglers, and always upstream. This is the first rule of their clubs and syndicates. It may stretch to cross-stream, and if nobody is about to just slightly downstream.

The dry fly needs a target. It is *possible* to fish with "the dry" if no trout are moving, though in less hope than with the wet.

You see the trout's ring on the water, you cast your dry fly just to the upstream edge of it. As the fly floats over the trout, it rises and swallows it.

Or perhaps not.

With dry fly-fishing, as with wet, you gather in the line with your left hand. But this is only to keep the line straight as the fly is borne downstream towards both the fish and yourself by the current. As the fly is resting on the surface, you cannot move it by your own force without imparting a wake which scares the fish.

This "drag" is a topic of headshaking concern to compleat anglers, as slicing and hooking to compleat golfers. Differing speeds of current on the surface can inflict drag on the flies of the most compleat ones. They counter it by casting skilfully upon the fast run of current — which intervenes between the calm holding the fish — a wobbly line any incompleat angler can achieve without the slightest effort.

(3) Nymphing is a very compleat form of angling.

It is performed upstream, and depends for its

success in recognizing when the trout opens and closes its mouth on the artificial nymph. It is thus beyond the incompleat angler, who has difficulty in recognizing a trout at all from a submerged log. But the incompleat angler chucking a nymph upstream is as likely to be rewarded by his luck as often as many compleat ones by their skill.

(4) Dry flies become damp, even when sprayed with silicone and false-cast in the air.

The tweeded generation squeezed them dry again with amadou, a brown tree fungus once used to dress wounds and staunch blood. Our unromantic generation uses an old handkerchief.

But even a dried dry fly begins to sink in fast and choppy water — like the flood from a partly opened hatch. This can afford the incompleat angler, baffled and frustrated by the skills of dry fly-fishing, the compensation of a catch. Drag is no problem when he is fishing on, or in, tumbling foam-flecked water. Damp fly-fishing is done by compleat dry fly-anglers only when the day is getting on and they have promised influential guests fresh trout for dinner.

* * *

The trout takes your fly. Your rod is bent. You look like a fly-fisherman, even from quite close.

What do you do?

You "Strike". This is a misleading compleat anglers' word which causes their incompleat comrades to jerk up their rod-tip as though opening an umbrella. This rips the fly from the mouth of the co-operative trout.

When you have a fish on the end, you simply tighten everything up. You raise the rod-tip a little, you hold the line firmly against the cork handle with your right forefinger. You take up any slack by pulling in the line with your left hand. This must become a reflex movement, a controlled transition from the relaxed to the secure grip, like grabbing the handrail if you stumble on the stairs.

Striking with the dry fly has a complication. The fish takes the fly in its mouth on the surface, but swallows it on its way under water. A delay must be made before tightening up, to avoid pulling the fly out again. Anglers are traditionally advised to time this agonized interval by shouting, "God Save the Queen".

All anglers have days when they fish better or worse than on others, just as we have days when our temper is sunnier or fouler than usual. The incompleat angler who infuriatingly finds that his small, hard-won skill has deserted him should continue fishing with the heartening reflection that many a good fish has been caught on a bad cast.

And be heartened more by the TENTH PRINCIPLE OF INCOMPLEAT ANGLING. *Most Fish Hook Themselves.*

* * *

You have your fish securely on the end of your

line. Now you play it.

To the compleat angler, this means letting it swim up and down under pressure. A trout will make eight to ten knots, about the same speed as a man on a bicycle (a salmon can touch twenty knots). The angler safeguards it from weeds, reeds, the piers of bridges, the anchor-rope of his boat, his own feet and other obstructions, until the fish is exhausted and turns submissively on its side.

The incompleat angler, in his excitement to get his hands on his fish, is more likely to inflict a tug-o'-war.

If the fish runs away from you, let out line after it. If the fish runs towards you, pull in line before it. Most anglers use the reel for this. But I have found that my clumsy incompleat fingers respond better to the fish's movement by the same mechanism that draws the wet fly through the water — holding the line against the cork handle with the right forefinger, altering the length of line by pulling in, or letting out, the slack controlled by the left hand.

Whenever playing a fish, in whichever direction it turns, always have the end of your rod bent in a good arc. Keeping this picture in mind under difficult circumstances — for instance, the trout swimming under your boat, or you falling into the water — will much reduce the anguish of losing a hooked fish.

Take care not to let the knot at the end of your line slip through the ring at the end of your rod. It will not slip back again, and severely restrict your room for manoeuvre.

If the fish sticks among weeds or reeds, put down your rod, take the line beyond the tip, and pull the trout steadily towards you. It is the same technique as pulling your fly out of a tree. When the trout is eased out of the weed by hand, and flashes away in another direction, this creates an interesting situation for the incompleat angler.

Do not try to net the fish too soon. The sight of the net frightens it into further struggles, and the angler with rod high above his head in one hand, net deep in the water against threshing trout with the other, is liable to lose both his fish and his balance. Before unclipping your net from your belt, wait until you feel that you can move the fish wherever you want to. Then draw it towards you, and slip the net under it. Do not take the advice of Izaak Walton, who would throw his rod into the water with a big fish, and collect both later.

Unhook the trout, holding it firmly behind the gills. Kill it by hitting its head on a stone. Some anglers use a "priest", which is a fish cosh.

Perhaps we should never kill fish. Perhaps we should never kill anything for sport. If angling is a brutal and brutalizing pastime, its amiable and gentle practitioners must be the best disguised of savages.

8
The Inner Angler

8

The messy episode of gutting his catch should follow as soon as possible the incompleat angler's triumphant return home. The flavour of trout left ungutted in the refrigerator even overnight becomes impaired with muddiness.

Do not ape the deft fishmonger with his knife. A sharp stout pair of scissors is less danger to your fingers. Perform the operation in the kitchen sink with a flow of cold water. If your fish is unattractively slimy, leave it in a bowl of salt water for a few minutes first.

Trout are cooked with the head on. This is to make plain to any guests that they are eating trout and not a herring. There is in addition plenty of meat at the back of the head and the brain is esteemed a delicacy, if found.

As the head is not amputated, the gills must be removed. Lift the gill cover, hook the gills forwards with your finger, and snip the bands retaining each end with your scissors.

Open the length of the belly with the scissors, and pull out the entrails under the flow of water.

Always scrape out the long dorsal vein with a finger-nail run against the backbone, or the trout will become discoloured and even distasteful when cooked. The trout will look prettier when served if you make the slit in its belly only an inch and a half long, at the rear end. You pull out the entrails with the help of a finger pushed through the spaces freed of the gills.

Never put your fingers in a trout's mouth. Though dead, its teeth are sharp and infective.

Gutting the trout is an opportunity for a little anatomy. Its dark red liver is obvious, so is its little pink heart. From the feel of its gut, you can tell if it has been eating crunchy snails and mussels. Compleat anglers stick little scoops down the throats of their dead fish, and pore over the stomach contents spread across a dish, as Roman soothsayers over the entrails of fowls. This is an interesting and rewarding investigation even for the incompleat angler, but you must restrain yourself from describing the absorbing discoveries to your guests who are enjoying their fish.

Trout can always be sexed, even in the earlier part of the season when spawning is far off. The female has bright orange, gritty ova, the male smooth pink milt.

The flesh of trout just out of the stewpond is white and insipid. When they have lived in a river or lake for a while, they become tastier and pinker. This salmon-pink flesh is not laid down by muscular activity in chasing the diet of a wild fish. It comes from carotine in the shrimps and snails which the trout swallows.

Small wild trout may be white in colour, but they are good to eat. Roll them in flour and fry them gently in oil and butter, or grill them brushed with butter. When the angler's increasing expertise is reflected in trout of three-quarters of a pound or more, different treatment is demanded.

A fish of this size is large enough to be baked. This is best done in an open dish on the middle shelf of a hot oven (Number Six Regulo, or 350 degrees Fahrenheit), for twenty-five to thirty-five minutes according to size. The dish must be fish shaped, or two-fish shaped if a brace is being cooked. The dish is buttered and the trout brushed with butter, but if the dish does not fit closely the butter runs away and burns. If you do not have a dish to match your fish, lay it in buttered foil.

But do not parcel it in the foil. Baking gives a crisp skin, lost if the foil or dish is closed. As an aromatic refinement, the belly may be stuffed with dried herbs.

You can tell when the fish is done by its eye turning opaque.

Truite au bleu is the classical trout dish. It is really poached trout, but has a sinister reputation, because the trout is believed to be boiled as live as a lobster. Some pricy restaurants are decorated with little tanks, in which the trout swim happily regardless of their doom. But as the trout is gutted before being sprinkled with vinegar and thrust into the bubbling *court bouillon,* life must be as extinct as with any victim hanged, drawn and quartered at Tyburn. Hollandaise sauce goes well with it.

Truite aux amandes is another classical dish. The trout is floured and fried in oil and butter, the almonds toasted separately and added.

Smoked trout, cold with horseradish sauce, or fresh and hot, is a popular finale to a trout's life. Tackle-shops sell portable Swedish smokers, which come with full directions. If used at home, put them well away from the living quarters. The smell of smoking trout lingers longer than paint or spilt beer.

Trout *pâté* is relished by the few gourmets who have come upon it. Cook the trout as you wish — baking in butter will do. Skin it and remove all the bones, even the small ones. Pound the flesh in a bowl, with a heavy wooden spoon or a pestle. Check again that even the most insignificant bones have been eliminated. Season well with black pepper and salt. Add lemon juice, one lemon for each three pounds of *original* trout. The angler will have weighted his catch carefully, and recorded the figure in his handsome leather-bound book.

Then weigh the *pâté*, and add half its weight of melted butter. Beat well. Adjust the seasoning, as the cookery books say. Pack it into a dish and keep it in the fridge. It freezes well. Its top may be decorated with an artistic representation of the fish by courtesy of which it appears on the menu.

Trout *pâté* is a good way of serving large, not very tasty, white-fleshed fish. It achieves an extra delicacy if made from smoked trout.

My wife provided these recipes. I hope that you enjoy them. I cannot bear the taste of trout, and have never eaten one in my life.

* * *

If you had always wanted to go fly-fishing but thought it would be too difficult, too troublesome, too expensive or too snobbish, I hope this book has changed your mind. Some compleat anglers may complain that I have made angling over-simple. They would be right. But there are plenty of other compleat anglers who make it too complicated. Which brings us to the—
ELEVENTH AND FINAL PRINCIPLE OF INCOMPLEAT ANGLING. *Men Enjoy Passing The Time by Talking a Great Deal of Amiable Nonsense About Angling, as Men Enjoy Passing the Time by Talking a Great Deal of Amiable Nonsense about Everything.*